T H E

18,000-TON

OLYMPIC

DREAM

OTHER BOOKS OF POETRY BY T. R. HUMMER

The Angelic Orders

The Passion of the
Right-Angled Man

Lower-Class Heresy

THE
18,000-TON
OLYMPIC
DREAM

POEMS

QUILL
WILLIAM MORROW
NEW YORK

Some of the poems in this book have been previously published and appear
with permission as follows:

Gettysburg Review: "Slow Train Through Georgia"; "Austerity in Vermont"
Georgia Review: "Bluegrass Wasteland"
The Journal: "Decorum"
Shenandoah: "Courtly Love"; "Green Mountain Fever"
Western Humanities Review: "Salt Flats Crossing: Homage to
Vachel Lindsay"; "The March Personifications"

Recognizing the importance of preserving what has been written, it is the
policy of William Morrow and Company, Inc., and its imprints and affiliates
to have the books it publishes printed on acid-free paper, and we exert our
best efforts to that end.

Library of Congress Cataloging-in-Publication Data

Hummer, T. R.
    The 18,000-ton *Olympic Dream* : poems / T. R. Hummer.
        p.   cm.
    ISBN 0-688-09018-4. — ISBN 0-688-09754-5 (pbk.)
    I. Title.   II. Title: Eighteen-thousand-ton *Olympic Dream*.
PS3558.U445A616   1990
811'.54—dc20   89-48525
                                                                   CIP

Printed in the United States of America

First Quill Edition

1 2 3 4 5 6 7 8 9 10

BOOK DESIGN BY BARBARA BACHMAN

FOR THEO

CONTENTS

I

THE 18,000-TON OLYMPIC DREAM

THE 18,000-TON
OLYMPIC DREAM

CORNWALL: WINTER, 1987

Ex nihilo,
      that's how it begins.
Light as consciousness: again the old story,
Hung in this muddy dawn like the memoryless
Denouement of a lifelong dream-series
The dreamer never even knows
He has to sleep through
                over and over,
And yet the scene takes shape—
Horizon, fog-depressed zenith, simplified contour
Of sea, curve of bay, wedge of slip, line of quay,
All reduced to its least common geometry
In this obscured warp
          of January morning.
North-northeast of St. Ives's seawall,
The old lighthouse is still invisible,
But any tourist could tell you
It certainly exists, years lightless
Maybe, granite-gray
            in its own
Irreducible right, but part
Of what minutes from now will have grown
Humanly enlightened enough for someone else
To call the visible world—
Things will firm up,
          clearly,
In some immediate future,
But not yet, not here
And now, not for me. St. Ives, asleep
In the neutral zone of its own self-forgetting,
Is colorless as what I remember
            of the sweep
Of TV cameras I saw tracking that swath
Of nothingness a disembodied voice
Called the Mediterranean,

Where the 18,000-ton *Olympic Dream*
Was going down. What memories
                              do the inland-born
Have of the archetype of drowning? Mine
Are black and white, blurred in the subliminal
Flicker and snow-grain
Of bad reception. The locus
Is the lobby of this cheap
                              St. Ives hotel,
With its worn-out Zenith set
And post-dated Christmas tree. Onscreen
The helicopter's focus
Shifted, caught, held,
And there, against
                              undifferentiated gray
Only the newscaster's spiel revealed
Was ocean, appeared the black list
Of the tanker *Olympic Dream*. She was sailing
From Kuwait for unnamed Western destinations,
Course clear, speed steady,
                              southern breeze
Self-evidently warm, when suddenly her hull
Broke open. That was last night. After the News,
I wandered calm into the steep
Emptiness of St. Ives, alone, and found
A bar where nobody asked me
                              where I'm from.
That was essential, I thought: to be unknown
And unrevealed in this part of the world
Where I'd come, vaguely ashamed
Of my country, of the language
I can't help speaking—
                              my voice
An indelible brand no amount of goodwill
Or cautious politics can hide: American. Now,
While day begins straining
The bay's fog, a myopic patina
Outside the window,
                              I am vaguely ashamed
Of my own shame's vagueness—
But last night I sat drinking, forgetting what I knew
In my dumb happiness. And after, a simple tourist,

I stumbled on stairs cut in the seawall. I descended,
And the visible world broke
                              out of the instressed
Narrowness of St. Ives's streets—
Cloud-scattered sky, full moon,
The deep-moiled windstroked
Opalescent midnight January Atlantic—
Water grained and hued like molten oak
                              moving
With that trite and mythic
Heart-shattering noise I can only dimly
Call *roar*—and the image came again:
Somewhere a thousand miles
South-southeast behind me—
                    no, closer—
The 18,000-ton *Olympic Dream* was foundering
In the widow-making unchilding unfathering
Sheet of television colorlessness
I was only just remembering.
There was fire,
                    the newscaster said,
And the image proved it: Smoke
Eclipsed what otherwise would be
A perfect layout from a perfect tourist pamphlet,
Rising from the peacefully tilted ship,
Rising from the sea
                    where crude oil veined
From her ruptured hold
And burned. Uncertain cause, prognosis
Unknown, as yet no casualties
Identified: Bitter ambiguities learned
By generations
                    of journalists struggling to name
Catastrophe, where in this moon-infected night
The ship still yielded to the same impersonal whir
Of videotape, releasing miraculous light
From the hold's black ballast
Toward helicopters,
                    into satellites—
Ground of being, and granite of it—past
Microwave towers, relay stations, the sludged-out
Windows of sleeping Europe, moving west

At the speed of light into self-consciousness's secret
Archive of the history of pain.
                                    How much can I tell
About the way I think? It's morning now, still pre-dawn—
Something's wrong with time, time's gone lyric—
And I've stared for hours over St. Ives Bay
Through this smeared hotel window,
Obsessively awake.
                            This is more
Than simple insomnia. This is one way
I try to prove to myself I'm somewhere, and alive.
I squint into the half dark. *Cornwall*,
I say, then *Ohio, Mississippi*.
What name can I believe?
                                    What difference does it make?
In the room adjoining mine, two friends obsessively sleep—
The couple from Virginia, come
Miles out of their lives, a New Year's trip
To visit me, their six-month expatriated
Fellow American.
                            Yesterday we drove
The glyphic shape of the north Cornish coast
In a rented car and in rain.
At the grim noon of a January gale,
We raised Tintagel, stupid enough
To climb those cliffs
                            in such a wind
And hold on to the lying Arthurian ruins,
Tourists of the terrible
Thrust and suck of ocean a hundred sheer
Feet down. Later, they felt the nausea—
Strange food,
                    stranger water—
Wordsworth's Revenge, we called it,
Emetic motion regurgitated intranquilly.
Somewhere in the far camera-distorted gray
Of the Mediterranean, crude oil cusps and spills.
My friends sleep off
                            their convalescence,
And I stare out at the hotel's vista
Of indeterminate bay. I believe she is real,
The *Dream*, all 18,000 self-destructing tons of her.

14

I believe in the image of her burning,
Her sick angle of roll,
                         the dark gray stain she makes
In the lighter gray of the air
As her fire consumes her own ugly suffusions.
But whose revenge can name me
The silence of her sinking?
The uncertainties of memory,
                         the confusions
Of the fiction of the known? To hell with that.
Man Thinking is the breached body of the West's
Olympic Dream. Last night I stood moonblind
On the seawall stairs, blinking
At the sudden breaking open
                         of the visible.
That was one extreme of one man's single life.
And at the other end of the oil-slick scum
Of ignorance I slide on, the idiot
Spectrum of myself, the burning *Dream*
Pillared toward a heaven
                         where satellites that can read
A license plate on a black limousine
In the parking lot of the Kremlin
Missed the part where the drowned sailor
Clutched the dragnet. In my vision
Of St. Ives Bay,
                the lusterless dead-lights
Of millionaires' yachts pitched and orchestrated
A story of the beautiful
Old World, a picturesque night
Of ocean pearled by the cloud-curdled
Circle of moon—
                transcendence,
Sublimity, whatever self-serving label I give it,
I stood there and sucked it all in.
Call it *expanding the visible*—
Isn't that what we do? Anything goes:
More light.
                18,000 tons' worth, Arabian oil
That burns off the sea as fast as it spills,
The newscaster says, an absolute
Self-consumption. And this is the morning

15

Of that darkness, these are the grays
I'm left with
                        until the sun burns,
As the TV promised, the chronic fog
Off Cornwall. But that's not good enough.
In the stop-time of this illusion
Of dramatic guilt, this pitiful
And suspicious effort
                        to be political, liberal,
I could say *My friends wake up,*
And the rented car, American,
Takes us west to Land's End,
Ourselves again, healed and whole:
And the hammerhead
                        and the oily gull
Would cede me their old dominion,
And the stars reflected in the firmament
Would slip degree by degree
Toward apocatastasis or oblivion,
Whichever comes first
                        or last, and the whole
Translucent shape of creation revealed
Through this blurred screen of hotel-room window
Would shiver, warp, rip,
And give away the whole miserable show—
One more lie
                        from me, one son of a bitch
In a universe at the mercy of sons of bitches
With bodyguards or mandates
Or Presidential Bibles, or Truth half baked
Like a bastard file in MacFarlane's sickeningly sweet
Key-shaped cake,
                        to which the whole third world
Replies, in the words of the prophet, *America,*
Go fuck yourself with your atom bomb.
I believe off the coast of Greece
The sky is shot
Gold with the full
                        radiance of dawn,
Or the doomed final color
Of an oil-slick burning off the sea, and nobody
Sees it, no helicopter journalist, no television zoom,

And certainly not me. The truth is, I
Don't seem quite right myself.
                              Come dawn,
I've lost my immunity. Wordsworth's Revenge.
St. Ives Bay lightens, and I feel
The visionary poison unsettle
In the pit of my belly. Cause and effect
Come down to this:
                    We are all still here,
Trapped in this description
Of the coast of beautiful historic Cornwall,
My sleeping friends and I, carriers holed up
In a budget-priced tourist bed-and-breakfast
With a certain view of the sea,
                              its winter obscurity,
Its shifting invalid ships—and, I've read,
An authentic and undeniably real
Lighthouse, ready to focus its grayness dead
In the middle of this fog
That will start to thin *ad nihilum*
                              any second now.

—for Greg Donovan and Tracy Trefethen

II

WORDSWORTH'S REVENGE

DECORUM

The man in the bedroom doesn't want to lie anymore.
He stands up and goes to the window. Outside,
Midwestern November rain is a mercuric sheen
Stippling the street, but no matter how he squints
He can't see it falling through the air. You try to know these
   things:
How all over town, dark divides itself meticulously from light,
How the eighteen wheels of a diesel raise a blinding steam off the
   bypass
To white your windshield out. All your life
You've heard of the middle of the night,
And here it is, suddenly, all you bargained for and then some.
So the meditation goes, but outside the window the world
Is closed as the face of a lover, coming.
He stands in the dark room, his body stained
The pale lavender of the streetlights. It has rained for weeks,
A slow, cold, naked rain. Nothing has happened. Nothing is going
   to happen.
He would open the window and let the lean shape
Of what wind there is come against him,
But he cannot imagine touching what he has no image for.
This is what it is like to believe in saying
Only what has to be said. This is what it is like to lose your story.
On another street, out of sight, a motorcycle makes
A sound like something profoundly breaking
High in the back of the neck, where the brainstem joins the spine,
And when the nerves let go, the body stops feeling.
He lays his hand on the window glass, imagines
The pinpricks of cold enter the bloodstream powerfully,
Veining toward the heart. He imagines this is the night
The angel comes due, and there is no lamb and no firstborn—
Nothing but his word, no acceptable sacrifice.

SPRING COMES TO MID-OHIO
IN A HOLY SHOWER OF STARS

On the clearest night of the earliest spring of my life,
An Easter Sunday, come in March by the luck of the draw,
I saw a streak of light in the sky like the middle finger of God,
But it did not come down on me. It was the brightness
William James heard about
                         from a housewife-turned-saintly-spiritualist
That she said she always saw when the dead were about to touch
    her
In that certain way the dead have. I saw it effloresce and vanish.
Standing there on the road next to the blacked-out body of an oak,
I wanted to trance myself into the past, to get in touch
With the ectoplasmic other side.
                         I wanted some strangeness to speak
Out of the unpragmatic crystal ball of my larynx and name itself,
In the timbre I whisper to lovers in, my life. But then another
Finger gestured godlike halfway down from the zenith, another,
    another,
And the sky burned with the print of a whole left hand.
That's the way the past works:
                     brilliance, and a slap in the face.
Years later, in winter, when the rusted iron wheels
Of snowplows gave their spiritual groans in the heat-dead
    midnight streets,
I would dream God's immaculate body could suddenly be struck
With a human palm the color of fever, and darken, and die.
But that night in mid-Ohio,
                     I knew what the housewife knew
When James sat in her dingy seance parlor with his notebook
    clumsy on his knee:
That nothing you ever dreamed of saying comes of its own free
    will.
It has to be beaten out of you, word by impossible word, until the
    dead
Spread themselves in your flesh like March dogwood spreads
    through the dark,
And you speak,
               and a stranger writes everything down.

UNSKILLED LABOR, RIVER CITY

What visible heat
            this water possesses moves
In submerged backwash between its surface and the mind
Of the foreigner who stands above it on the bridge.
The river is brown and wide and the city staggers
Around it on the slopes
                of its mother hills.
New Orleans, Manhattan, London, Paris, Rome—
The lineage goes as deep as what we remember
Of history, all the vaguely known facts
We think of as *Tigris* and *Ganges*.
                      Let's say this is a town
In central California, and the one on the span
Is a woman who has left her passport home,
Her children. She stands here beginning
To see how river-light
            can shiver between
This water and the Sierras, obscuring
The walls of a broken mission—
Undercliff adobe shading a shallow crater,
All that remains
           of the mass grave of Indian slaves
Who wattled it, dead of smallpox now
Two hundred thoughtless years. Or call it a seedy
County seat in eastern Mississippi,
Say the man on the bridge
               owns nothing
But a guitar case and the razor in his boot.
This is where the bus will come,
And the driver who'll call him *nigger*,
This is where the road
            forks north
To Chicago and another river. The beauty
Of the archetype of the river city is
That you don't have to choose. You can have it both ways,
You can have it a million ways at once:
               It coexists

In space and time and the mind of everyone
Trying to remember where it came from,
What it took to call so much wood and stone and earth
Into bodies
                    we tell ourselves we know
As *bridge* and *city*. The man with the razor sweats
In the lash of this July heat,
But the woman has half forgotten
The pain that cut
                    its valley through her cervix
And took on the flesh of a daughter and a son
Who return to her now in memory
Rainbowed with bloody oil, stained as I am with the passage
Of steel-screwed ships
                    blown from the heart
Of industrial oceans—off course, listing
With their commerce of enslavement,
Drawn, let's say, like the needles of sensitive compasses,
Or certain as gods
                    to break us down and sail on.

COURTLY LOVE

The candle in the bathroom burns all night
And water in the clawfoot bathtub cools.
It is simple as that. It is clear
This man and woman are lonely and love each other.

Let's say each washed the other clean,
Each lay the other naked
And half asleep on the thick white rug
In the high-ceilinged room of the empty old house

Where I can't help making them lie,
Where in the word *night*
Outside the casement windows
Rain on oak limbs suddenly turns to ice—

As if any of this were more
Than something someone thought of saying,
More than a dream of lost words
We are living through,

The story that goes on being
Mumbled behind the thick,
Old-fashioned plaster of the walls
Of a mind we all share, that tries

Again and again to wring out of me
What those older, other lovers
Must have done when they woke stiff
And dew-cold in a forest

With the king her husband's unexpected sword
Between them like the bitter body
Of a child—he rode up while they slept
And laid it there in memory

Of certain honorable truths. But not enough
Remains of the unlikely off-center ballad

They had to sing to make sense of
Except the white façade

Of this house in mid-Ohio
That fronts a streetful of pickups hissing
Their all-weather tires on the ice,
Conditionally real as the bathroom floor

Where the ancient heraldic lion-footed tub
Spreads its porcelain claws
Beside the blanked-out bodies
Of the two who stir on the white rug now in candlelight,

Dreaming maybe, or—as if the flesh
Of the Western world has a right
To print its darkening
Story on the white page of itself—

In pain a little, a little bruised
Where touch turned to a desperate holding on.

THE MIST TREES
VANISH INTO

On this first morning of the grayness of winter, the wind
Lets its invisible body take on the thickness
Of a sick man trying to think. The images come hard.

This is late December in Ohio, where everything
We believe we know is a little dim, a little
Hazy to the touch. Through the steamed double glass

Of the office window, rain-bleached trees lose their edge
In the indiscriminate air of our native country,
Where, yes, the hardworking succeed

In working hard. This is working. This is the morning
We lift our coffee cups and start to take
Ourselves apart. This is the white-collar job

Our mothers never had, our grandfathers had no name for.
Out there, in the far corner of the parking lot,
The sky dumps an essence the color of pleurisy

On the working man's car, congesting
What vision anyone might have of the country
Beyond, the tended row of hardwoods, the roll

Of Ohio hillside—not farmland: open acreage, artificial,
Ornamental. Wasted? That depends on who you think you are.
But I tell you this is the season of the deepest

Subjective breathing, of air with an influenza stink
So thick you dream of the asthma your mother steamed
Out of your body, strangely the size of a child's,

The vaporizer by your bed lifting all night a blinding
Aura of Vicks. You take it into yourself again and again
Until you wake up grown in December, in Ohio, not knowing

How you got here, not caring that the wheeze of the old
Case tractor on a hillside out of sight
Is the Mississippi ghost of your grandfather, lost in worry

About weather, about what the earth still yields.
There's no end to this. Come spring, dogwood will spread
Purposely white against this other color—white

As a grandfather's chest under the heavy khaki shirt he wore
Summer-long against what cancer the sun
Might touch him with: white as the whole family in black

Around his grave the winter he died, drowned
In his own lungs' fluid: white as this paper we scatter
Our desks with, remembering the white man's burden,

Cotton in the fields, the high whorl of summer cirrus clouds
Crystalline as a hit of pure and precious cocaine
In the southern sky's clear-breathed blue where I sweated one

Like a man on the riveting back of a tractor. Come spring,
Crocus will open itself and die in late Ohio snow, revealed, and
    the air
Won't clear, the air will go on tincturing

The trees, and the spaces between the trees, and the space
    between
The trees and the window with the colorlessness
Of this present that chokes what believes it ought to be

The great white heart of the country I will die in
On a day in December, maybe, when the *pneuma* can't go on
    anymore
And all the trees disappear.

THE MARCH
PERSONIFICATIONS

Rain-touched, fields of winter-clodded loam
Dissolve in the alley back of the liquor store,
Memory turning everything inside out.
It is late afternoon, a Saturday, and the sky lays down
A clean patina of mist on the lids of the garbage cans.
This is a shortcut from downtown to uptown, the way
Winos have blazed with the crumbs of shattered empties.
Concrete glitters, shard-constellated, and I walk
With the care of the unreconstructed among alien holies of holies.
There's a garbage strike, and something rich in the air
Makes that overworked spark jump from ganglion to ganglion,
The mental stroke we've taught ourselves to call *association*:
Against the gray horizon, rusted tractors move,
Chisel-plows rip the peaty smell of leftover rot
Out of the just-thawed earth, and my uncle and my father
Stand on the turnrow watching, passing a flask.
It might be a miraculous vision of the other world
The dead find their torturous way to, but I believe
It is the dregs of love in the brain, and I try to hold on
To the distant barrage of the tractor, the bourbon aura
My father's breath becomes, the color of khaki workshirts
Darkened by the wet air of March and twenty-five wasted years—
But it falls apart like a bad metaphor, like a muffler
Tied to the frame of a car with a piece of coathanger wire
Until the whole ugly business rusts to pieces,
And you throw it in an alley where a stranger kicks it
Against a garbage can. The whole afternoon
Echoes that sickening thud, not the clear ring of true emptiness.
The old patriarchal world, the old lie of the derelict self
Degenerate here, and the stranger in the residue
Fumbles the brown bag from under his arm,
Slips out the bottle, breaks the seal, and takes
One small hit of cheap whiskey, to let its chemical bite
Of faintly tinted back alley peatsmoke take him farther down
Toward the shattered edge of the rain, the place he came from.

THE AUGUST POSSESSIONS

All over Wells, Nevada, numinous desert light
Shivers on the casinos' façades—pink fake adobe,
Neon, snakeskin—and big cars from Dallas and Jersey collapse

Sunstruck over the grease pit of the local Texaco.
At the motel desk they give us a roll of quarters,
Slapped in the palm with the heft of a good blackjack.

Enjoy, they say. And what else is there to do?
Everybody here is a lover, everybody has a secret key
To a bed they've never seen before, everybody has hope,

Even the room-service waiter, a skinny man born south of Juarez
Where his youngest sister died foaming a demon from her mouth
Before the priest could come. At noon, when the stalled sun

Raises a coma of heat waves off the parking lot,
He runs from room to room with his heavy tray,
Then hides on break in the everlasting

Twilight of the lounge where drivers of ruptured Lincolns
Wait for shipments of gaskets from Denver.
All of us here know the odds, but the waiter

Takes my elbow, shakes my hand
Off the handle of the slot machine I've fed ten dollars.
He has no papers, his spine has the subtle twist

Of *in utero* malnutrition, but I follow him
To the end of the row, to a machine like all the rest.
This, this, he says, and lays his graceful hands

On the jaundiced lemons of its eyes.
He was twelve years old when his father came in with the priest.
They wiped the epileptic sputum from his sister's face,

Burnt incense and prayed to keep the devils out
Long enough to bury her. No one but Jesus himself
Could promise them more. I balance my chances,

Drop in five quarters, pull the lever, and nothing comes.
The waiter shrugs. *The will of God*, he says,
Why listen to me?

Later, in the dark motel room, the common bed of many strangers
Strains, springs chording under the woman's body
Like tight barbed wire. I touch her face, and I find it

All again, the terror of the random fall
Of money, the leverage of percentages, the unapproachable
Whine of a border-patrol airplane, the voice

Of a priest with an ascetically grotesque body
And the hands of an angel commanding me, from the other side
Of the beautiful flesh I have come into, *Begone*.

SALT FLATS CROSSING:
HOMAGE TO VACHEL LINDSAY

The one American Poet who could sing out doors.—V. L.

At one hundred Fahrenheit degrees, the language loses
All its consonants. At one hundred ten,
Even the vowels begin to slip.
What you're left with is a voice like a sterno drinker's

When the throat gives in to the poison of the years.
What good will rhythm do you then?
West of Salt Lake City, the untranslatable hieroglyphic residues
Of old Lake Bonneville make their glittering scrawl—

Miles and miles of nothing but acres and acres
Of the white-hot wake of geological time. Look behind you,
My country, my virgin land, and you suddenly turn
To a mythical surface of salt, the locus

Of God's writer's block, the white page even he couldn't crack.
Across the mountains' enjambment, in the Valley,
Brigham Young said, *This is the place,*
And the desert, the Mormons will tell you, blossomed like a rose—

But this pseudo-snowscape was never anybody's place.
Anything rendered here is written in the tongue
Of the ancient godless wars of the acids and alkalis, whose
Chemical hatred subscends the first and the last

Gropings of understanding, human or divine.
Everyone stops short, or goes around, or is only passing through.
To the west is Las Vegas, St. Francis of San Francisco,
The Caesarian scar of the San Andreas Fault,

Thunderclouds of grapes hanging on the Sierra Madres, every one
A bona fide promised land—and east, of course,
Is everything real.
In the arable land of the Americas, flowers burst like bombs.

Here, nothing bursts except radiator hoses, gone
Dangerously soft as the back of the palate
In the unutterable heat of this whiteness. Nothing but salt
To the horizon, nothing but salt to the wound, the heart,

Inhuman, not the residue of the visionary sweat
Of patriarchs or abandoned alkies purifying liquid blindness
Through the vault of a black felt hat: Here
We are stunned by the salt of the lost American

Sea that might have drowned Manifest Destiny if the continental
  plates
Had given the slow bump and grind of their tactical shifting
A rhythm politically correct.
But what are the radical slogans of the natural world?

What are the populist politics of sodium?
Which way am I traveling here?
The vacant parallel lines of this four-lane highway
Point east, point west, meet at each horizon.

Nothing with a sense of human direction
Can survive long in between. Driving here, I can believe in
  anything,
A mirage taking shape in the heatwave–personified air
Over the highway a mile in front of me,

A Salvation Army band of angels coming between the Alpha and
  Omega
Of the boundaries of the visible, waving laser-bright trombones
And tambourines full of omnipotent silver dollars, the spooks
Of all the forgotten prophets and politicians who ever believed

In music men could march to, sonic-booming the beat
Of their bad bass drums sea to shining sea—
Lincoln, Teddy Roosevelt, Atgelt, Bryan, waving banners of beaten
  gold
Where the cherubim of reason have etched their one indelible truth

With infinity's acid: *All*
Political conviction should be based on a disciplined hatred

Of death. But I strain my eyes and nothing real is there
Beyond the desolate wind-gouged smear

Of the floor of vanished Lake Bonneville and the volume of Utah
   sky
That once held water where brontosaurs swam with the wordless
Elegance of armies—raising, I imagine,
White surf down the long strange coast as their bodies lifted

Against each other in ridiculous outsized love,
Too beautifully huge to survive
The countersong of chemistry already humming in the helix
Of the DNA, in the water, in the stars: simple elements,

The half lives, the dead stretches
That reel into distances, the cosmic rays, the inert gases,
The marching masses, the Lysol thickness of blood failing into salt
To which no throat that lives can ever be open long.

—for John Ward

SLOW TRAIN THROUGH GEORGIA

The mist that rises from this river solidifies the air
Underneath the rusty trestle where a train has come and gone.
It is the precipitate of the chemical morning, dumped
Unceremoniously into the clear solution of a summer night.
Hours earlier, the midnight freight detonated under starlight
Three hours late and thundering toward Birmingham, the red glow
Of the steel mills, the tincture of that constant dawn.
But now the air shuts down. Now the distant whistles of the
    morning shift
Into the throats of mockingbirds, and the sun works
Its electrolytic clarity from the top down, starting with the ozone.
The mist rising off the muddy little river curves south beyond the
    bridge,
Following the water, of which you might be tempted to imagine
It is the astral body, downstream toward the Gulf—
Because you want to believe in the soul of the river, don't you,
You want a name and a positive destination
For this ghostly swath like a scar between banks of new-leafed
    oaks,
As if the world had a center and you were standing in it,
As if everything turning were your own self-evident revolution.
But watch this scene long enough and the sun
Will defeat you, the beautiful obscurity of the mist
Will dilute and disappear. Already the revelation is working
Its inevitable way toward you from the upper atmosphere. Soon
The oil-scummed image of the surface of the river will superimpose
Its visionary dreariness on what you can see of the earth:
Red clay, a distant cotton field, the tin roof of a tenant house
Where morning touches a mirror and moves at the constant speed
    of light
To touch the face of the sleeping man who stirs and touches his
    wife
Who is awake already, worrying over breakfast, remembering
The deep-night noise of the train that stopped
Whatever dream she might have had, the double blackness

Of coal-heaped gondolas hours after midnight, the anonymous
  steel
Of wheels against greased rails, inhuman, turning—like everything
  she knows
About God and politics—against her, going nowhere.

MISSISSIPPI 1955
CONFESSIONAL

It would have been, I think, summer—it would have been August,
    I think,
Somewhere near midway between solstice and equinox,
When the tractors move all daylight in mirages of their own
    thrown dust
And the farmhands come in the back gate at noon, empty, with
    jars in their hands.
Imagine yourself a child with a fever, half delirious all that month,
And your sisters lift you in your white wooden chair, carry you to
    the edge
Of a hayfield, set you down in hedgerow shade and leave you
While they go into woods to turn, you think, into swans—
They are so lovely, your sisters, in their white sundresses
That appear and disappear all afternoon among the dark trunks of
    trees.
None of this ever happened. But remember the body-heat of the
    wind
As it came from behind the tenant shack just there on the eastern
    border
Of your vision to touch you with its loving nigger hand? And there
    you are,
A white boy brought up believing the wind isn't even human, the
    wind is happy
To live in its one wooden room with only newspaper on the walls
To keep out what this metaphor won't now let me call the wind—
But don't worry about that, your sisters in the woods are gathering
Beautiful fruit, you can hear it falling into their hands,
And the big pistons of the tractors drive thunderously home into
    cylinders.
Steel-bright as the future. You are five years old. What do you
    know?
Your fever is a European delicacy, it burns in your flesh like fate,
A sign from God, cynosure, mortmain, the intricate working out
Of history in the life of the chosen. O listen, white boy, the wind
Has a mythic question only you can answer: *If all men were brothers,*
Would you want your sister to marry one? Let me tell you, white boy,
    the wind

37

Is in the woods with its cornmeal and its black iron skillet,
It's playing its blues harp in the poison oak where your youngest
    sister,
The one with hair so blonde you think it looks like a halo of rain,
Is about to take off her dress. You sit there dreaming your mild
    fever dream.
You tap your foot to the haybaler's squared rhythms. They've
    dressed you in linen.
From the woods where your sisters lie suddenly down, you burn,
    snow-white.
I've seen your face. I remember your name. I prophesy something
    you can't imagine
Is coming to kiss you. And you thought I was reaching back to you
    in words
To tell you something beautiful, like *wind*?

POEM IN THE SHAPE
OF A SAXOPHONE

Refracted through years, this neon light comes back,
Blue in the etched lines of a bar's lead-glass windows.
Somebody in an apartment, high
Over the asthmatic August streets of one more city
In the whipped-out heart
                    of the old northeast,
Tries to make the horn sound sweet, like Hawk.
That's hip to know, who he wants to sound like,
What it is in his jaw that trembles a little wrong
Back of the reed—but the woman on the barstool knows.
She is a woman I loved
                 for what she remembered
About the breath, how if you don't move it
Exactly right the tones won't round, how the tongue
Has to do what it has to do precisely.
Now she sits on a barstool in the past, where I put her,
Blowing a smoke ring
                   delicately stained with the predictable
Bloodred lipstick of the early 1940s.
I put her there and I keep her there,
Dressed in blue silk she would never have chosen herself,
Years before she was born. I want her to hear the stillborn
Choruses waffle over
                the apartment window ledge and down
Into the street, into the bar where she sits, theme music
From a bad old movie. I want her there so I can speak of her
In the past tense, where it's safe, where nobody cares
If I say *I loved*, or if the horn in the high window lifts
Its minor third a shade
                indecorously sharp.
Her hair in this light takes the tone of brass, sweeps
Its unnatural metallic curve past her shoulder, cheap,
You'll say, and easy, but you don't understand
The timbre of love, gold in this nonexistent air,
The uterine mouth
               of the horn's bell where the tune crowns
And comes out crippled, a clubfoot kid with a kickball,

An old man blowing a blues-harp at the mouth of the subway.
This is how I imagine the place where I keep her,
The organized violence I commit on ordinary space.
This is what men and women
                              do to each other: make
Breathy worlds and expect each other to live there,
Beautifully improvised. This is why
When the light comes down blue from the neon sign
Sketched in the dry shape of a cool martini
To touch the gin in her glass,
                              it wavers off-key
And she frowns, she stubs out her cigarette,
She pays her tab and goes home, knowing where she's going,
Slow-dancing into some present where her husband and children
Listen to whatever music the stereo spins,
Where the houses love wants
                              stagger along the made-up
Streets of the suburbs, lawn by sunlit lawn—
And just as she's out of range, the man
With the horn overhead takes another breath, touches
The reed with his tongue, lays his hands
On the keys.
              Now, at street level, light comes down
In final abstract perfection on the right side of lovers
Walking perpendicular to what I will first call
Sunset, then blackout, Saturday night
Where the man upstairs touches the unreal gold
Curve of the horn's cold body,
                              starts counting time.

AUSTERITY IN VERMONT

Astral blue of old mountains, ridge after rising ridge
Blurring the western horizon just after the sun goes down,
And there, up five degrees, the cold yellow evening star
My almanac says will be Saturn this month, the bastard god
   nobody
Wants for a father—not much light, but it's all Vermont conceives
Now that September's come and I feel like losing weight.
What is this voice I hear that tells me *Less flesh?*
Where does it go, the meat of the belly, when I stop
Drinking beer and run my groaning mile a day
Into the Yankee wind that articulates a whole
Future of frost in the darkening perpendiculars of maples?
All flesh has a fate, sure enough, though it's clear no body believes
This moment's horoscope, Saturn in the sixth house descending,
Pissed-off cannibal planet of constipation and infanticide—
But what can you do if you're being born right now
In a ward in Burlington? They're about to cut the cord
Just as that point of luminescence the color of urine on snow
Crowns at the lip of the sky's birth canal. Will you scream
At the doctor to wait just five minutes more with his surgical steel—
Hold on, get back until that terrible light tips over the edge
And dissolves into somebody else's birthday? But look,
It's too late, there's a snip and you're bleeding, your flesh
And your mother's are suddenly lives apart,
And there you lie, naked in that planet's damning radiation.
That's how destiny works—you'll never be a stockbroker,
You'll have five kids of your own, you'll live on a farm in Vermont
Rolling stones up a hill for years until one afternoon you come
   home
And open fire with your old shotgun on everybody in sight.
Right at the moment, gasping for air, I'm trying to remember
How it felt when the doctor shagged me loose from the rope of
   blood
That strained me down toward the good sleep of the placenta,
And I was myself apart, zapped from a dozen angles
By all the essences of my future—Mercury, Venus, Mars,
The whole merciless pantheon of necessary acts

That impressed themselves in my blue flesh turning red
With its own bloody weight. And look at me now,
Out on a road in Vermont at sunset, running, trying to choose
To make the bulge in my belly disappear the way my mother's did
After the lying-in, after the labor, after the voice
In the anesthetic stopped its mindless song, and some stranger
Lay there beside her with a body already growing
Ascetic, unbelieving, refusing her, demanding nothing not its own.

GREEN MOUNTAIN FEVER

On a ridge above Lake Pleiad, the fresh Caesarian scar
Of a ski slope meanders through the proud flesh of massed
    autumn maples,
Bringing back the old mother-lie of the earth's bulge—
What was ever born here?—as the mountains metastasize
Their redness in the hydrogen light of another Vermont October
    afternoon.
Here is a place you can freeze and burn just walking
In and out of shadows, in and out of the wind.
The books say love will be like this, all symptom, untreatable,
But something will come of it, something like what I saw
Years ago in a pulp magazine—*Spontaneous Human Combustion*,
    caption and photo
Of a homey green armchair, cloth etched black with the crude
Unmistakable shape of a human body, clear as on a Nagasaki wall.
    True,
That magazine called itself. I believed. I still want to believe.
I walk softly in this zenith-light, taking my body filled
With phlogiston and napalm gently up the trail to the top of the
    ridge
Where the ski-lift platform cantilevers over the frost-burnt slope
Down which, after first snow weeks from now, lovers and fools
    will throw
The bombs of themselves, and something will come of it—
    snow-blindness,
Adrenaline, unconsciousness, deliverance, broken bones, the quick
Joy of the body, a child born years from now on a January day
In the C-section ward of a southern city where everyone looks up
Suddenly when the snow begins and they have to learn to breathe
Its small quick blades and then heal themselves scarless and sterile.
But I'm wrong. That was all years ago. That was all true.
Now I can stand alone on this platform with its perilous scenic
    view
And tell myself it's a lie, nobody just explodes, it always takes
    longer:
Heat and light, yes, but blood too, and the amniotic fluid, and the
    father-guilt,

43

And the needle that exorcises peritonitis, and the needle that tries
  to heal
The uterus and all the intricate layers of muscle and flesh and skin
That, turned inside out, release, yes, a human shape—
And you give it a name that lets you love it like your own—
And that's when the fever starts. So now the body heat
Of the mountains rises and falls, and I stand watching the haze
In the distance clarify as the wind makes its incision,
And when the shadow of a cloud comes over me, I say the names
  of it all—
Vermont, Green Mountains—as if something could come of the
  saying,
As if that were a cure, as if just by believing it I could make
The blood in my heart boil to a fine October vapor,
My flesh incandesce in a gestalt of pure oxidation,
And vanish off this mountain absolute and clean, never leaving
Another scar in the shape of myself anywhere in the world again—
That much, you'd think, I could do in the name of love.

—for my daughter

NEW ENGLAND
BAD CONSCIENCE

This terrible personalness, this post-midnight in early winter,
Comes over me with its scrim of pearlescent clouds and insistent
    moon.
With the hands of my heart, as Augustine says, I brush these
    things away:
But they resist, remain. So much for the power of the heart,
So much for the strength of the hands, so much for the grip—
So much I give up and get up, leave the narrow Puritanical bed
That radiates November from the spoked iron arc of its head and
    foot.
I dress myself in wool and denim and down and go out where it
    all persists,
An ordinary exercise in trying to sleep, no mystery here. I take
My dreamless body into the sky-curdled morning, where
The icy residues of yesterday's snow silver-plate the schematic
Silhouettes of trees. I walk through the neighborhood, its windows
    still
Innocent with the darkness I can't give in to, every consciousness
    behind
Every curtain and valance and blind blacked out or transformed
    into strange
Landscapes of irresponsible desire in which everything visible is
    part of the dreamer
And thus lifted beyond the reach of the laws of the body into a
    narcissism so pure
It won't even be remembered when hours from now the alarm
    goes off
And the blankets roll back in the light. East and west of me, the
    mirror-image steeples
Of Catholic and Baptist churches go on with their old reflexive war:
Theory and practice, the City of God, the address of the soul after
    death.
With the hands of my heart, says Augustine. *The hands of my heart.*
Beyond frost-diamonded lawns I turn right for the town's silent
    center
Where shop windows hold in their overpriced sweaters and tourist
    corkscrews

But reveal on their other, outer faces the other, outer face of the
   moon.
Reflection: Isn't that what I'm here for? Reflection and conscience
   and sleep?
I stop on the bridge above this small Vermont town's small
   Vermont river,
Stuck in all the clichés it converges: river as metaphor
For life and death and everything in between, river as Self, river as
   Other,
River as unconscious reality that doesn't give a damn
What any mind thinks it means. Mercurial water slips black and
   silver
Over a spillway. Mist goes up, freezes on stones, on low maple
   limbs,
Freezes freestanding in November air and falls. I hear the heavy
   meter
Of the water's circulation. I hear my own breath go. I look up for a
   pattern
Of stars, but the moon in its tissue of cloud occludes what I need
   to see:
That self-consuming. *With the hands of my heart.* The river
Has one mist, the sky another—obscurity reflects obscurity, over
   and under.
But the town surrounds me with its constellation of blacked-out
   lives gone down
To the iron cold of selflessness, pure as suicide. I touch
The bridge rail, the tremble river water makes as it transmigrates
Into that fated ventricular emptiness the blood in my hands
   remembers.
I brush these things away.

A HEART ATTACK IN
THE COUNTRY

Something is shattering high in the frozen
Twilight pines. It makes a weightless rattling
Like layers of isinglass in the window
Of an antique woodstove, brittle with years
Of inward flaming, finally letting go.
The postcard vistas of Vermont collapse
With the icy weight of this moon's condensation,
This circumscribed sky's breaking down its old
Familiar persona with murderous transparency,
Arcing toward blackness and the poisonous
Chromates of starlight. In the valley
That disappeared half an hour ago
Under the shadow of a minor mountain,
The coroner's house radiates its porchlight.
Twenty miles northwest, in Burlington,
Post-rush-hour headlights constellate
The street in front of the shabby red-brick
County morgue where he left the body
Half dismantled at quitting time. Nights like this
There's a border in the air nobody can see
Where the inner and outer bleed into each other
Painlessly: What death by drowning ought to be
But probably isn't. Who knows? It's just
One more landscape when you go down,
Just one more expanse of one damned thing
Next to another. But this steady sound
High in the growing blindness of the air
Is a tinnitus like the detonation
Of nitroglycerine in the blood,
A scraping of ice against ice.
The woman turned herself inside out for him.
Caucasian female, he wrote on the chart, *sixty-five*.
Scalpels for the belly-flesh, a small bright saw
For the sternum: A layman can hardly imagine
The sounds in an insulated room
When the doors of the body open.
In that interior space, a textbook order appears:

Contour of stomach, liver, spleen, one lung
Laid next to another. All these things remain
Defined as long as the darkness holds
Everything up on the curve of its surface tension,
Keeps clear the veins and meridians
Of this night, still glazed with the afternoon's
Freezing rain. Pines arrange themselves in icy
Starlight outside the room where the woodstove glows,
Where the man stares down at his sterile hands
As they lay out the cutlery, the plates.
Cause of death, he wrote: *Congestive heart failure,*
Massive. Sleet rattled on the windows
Of the morgue all afternoon. He cut
The ruptured heart loose, raised it like a newborn
Into the artificial whiteness of surgical arclight.
Buy coal, he wrote at five o'clock, as February twilight
Made its professional incision in the tissue
Of clouds, and the mercury went down. Tomorrow,
He knows, the body will be the same, all cause
And consequence, a naked arrangement
Of temporary questions. Here, over his honed roofbeam,
Over the driveway where his car is parked,
Over the aureole of the mountain, the arbitrary track
Of a meteor slits the sky between the breasts from groin to throat.
What sound does it make, cutting through
That elevated breathlessness? Such silence is specialized
Knowledge a layman can hardly imagine, no matter
How the evening sky sharpens its clarities.

POLITICS

First the wind warps
                    the water oaks, skewing the season toward spring.
Then the body heat of the night breaks its palpable design
And lightning back of thunderheads discharges the transfixing
    power
That flickers in the temporal lobes of a *grand mal* epileptic.
I come downstairs and feel
                         the season tremble in the rotting
Porch boards of the dying small-town house I pay my little rent
To live in, uncertain I or anyone belongs here, a failure of faith
On the order of any saint's dark night of the soul, only stranger.
In the black sky off to starboard,
                            lightning branches and rebranches and dies
Like the pattern of genealogy in a Presbyterian's family Bible,
But nothing my mother ever found in her obsessive sifting
Through the inky residue of the bloodline of our name is written
    there.
When the thunder peaks, the whole
                            street opens and echoes
The origin of revelation in the breakdown of the syntax of prayer.
The hard thing is not to stop. The hard thing is to take it further,
And to hell with nature if it comes to that, and the backside of the
    hand of God:
I am one man of millions here,
                            one measure of flesh and breath,
And no hidebound book and no wind-warped water oak can wash
The blood-smell off me, no violence of rain can render me
Mystic, ascetic, solitary, any name you care to give
                            the arrogant and alone.

III

BLUEGRASS WASTELAND

WITH APOLOGIES

Bob Cantwell and Bob Bernard

and to Johnny
the mandolin player
for the Flat Mountain Boys
of Stillwater, Oklahoma,
who squinted down from the bandstand
at the Wild Willy's Bar crowd
and muttered into the microphone
*Ain't nothing out there, friends,
but a bluegrass wasteland.*

I

In Louisiana summer, hurricanes lift
Their unpersonifiable vastnesses out of the Gulf of Mexico
And hammer into the mainland, looking for no one.

The boy sits in a tall chair staring out a plate-glass storm door
Onto the brick patio where rain shivers canna leaves to pulp.
A book lies open in his lap, a cheap old edition

Of Jules Verne's 20,000 Leagues Under the Sea.
From it an odor rises of disuse and loneliness,
Of the sweat of spinster librarians and antiseptic dust.

He found it on a high shelf of the local parish library
Where nobody had touched it in years, no names on its card,
And brought it to his grandmother's house to sit reading alone

Of the madness of Captain Nemo. The book's spine creaks
As the storm takes shape over the Gulf. Outside the round
Crystal window of the Nautilus, unimaginable creatures move.

When the boy grows up, he will remember only vaguely
The submarine's interior, the characters' names, the action:
But the lonely crazy old man who played the pipe organ deep undersea

Will have a definite face in his mind, a distinct voice.
And he will remember the storm, how the earth-colored urns
Planted with succulents on the patio keep blurring in rain.

Why should any of this seem sad? In some future, it will all assume
The lineaments of high tragedy, the captain and his beautiful
Miraculous homemade machine, the broken leaves on the bricks,

The cheap iron-black patio furniture quicksilvered with storm.
Where will it all be going? It is all going down,
Derelict wreckage, sinking, spun

54

In the vortex of hurricane. Now, as he looks through the glass,
It becomes a dull ache of excitement he will one day think he understands
Is sexual. But even that will be wrong, only a word that means

As much as Mozart would mean if you heard that music played
From deep underwater while you floated in a lifeboat
Terrified, praying for rescue, singled out, cannibal.

We choose how to begin. We choose touch
In a dark room, alone. We choose nakedness
Come by the hard way, and slow.

There is the deliberate awkwardness
Of clothes, the motion, the time it takes
To take them off,

Not the way we like to imagine them
Simply disappearing in a cinematic dissolve:
They cling. They demand

To be consciously removed.
The pale slow uplift of pullover wool
Holds on to the woman's breasts.

Even in this dark, I see them rise,
Fall, released. Now there should be
Some beautiful image coming

Out of all this circumstance,
Out of our being here, out of our bodies,
But it would be a lie to say

Whiteness, calyx, lip
Of snow, lip of blood.
If there is going to be suffering

There must be an authority for pain.
Touch me is all I can tell you.
There is no true or adequate story.

Outside, moonlight calcifies the asphalt
And two station wagons parked in the shadow
Of a gut-rotted crabapple tree. Even here, where a side street

Arcs by a parking lot, if you want pure nature, all you have to do
Is look straight up. No matter what's on the moon, what's in the
   air,
That ought to be enough for anyone.

A convertible drifts by, discolored by moonlight and arclight,
Roof up, window rolled down a crack, bluegrass on the radio:
Blue moon of Kentucky, keep on shining:

And nobody thinks a thing about it,
Nobody connects it to anything, until
In the dark office, the man and woman prepare

To begin making love. Later, they will both remember it
Absurd and sad—in an office, in a room without a bed,
Silhouettes of typewriters, telephones, file cabinets

Hard-edged in what passes for that room's darkness,
Somebody's report half-written and glowing
On the desktop like moon-suffused snowlight—

But neither will say it to the other, ever.
You could name everything here—*desk lamp, ledger,*
Pocketbook, car key, pavement, crabapple, moon—

And never be outside nature, never even begin
To get beyond the clear hard perfection
Passion flowers into from its root word *pain.*

They don't understand. They touch and they go on touching.
In the dark, they have voices, wordless but real.
They touch and the voices begin: touch, and begin again.

Now things get dangerous. Consciousness floats free.
Shaken loose from first person, the voice can say anything.
All sorts of pernicious illusions come to mind:

The cinematic illusion, say, where the language rises
Against the reader's imagination like images on film—
Or is it images on a screen?—and assumes that authority

Of instantaneous occurrence, *comme ça*:
Frame: through a Cyclone fence, two Ford station wagons
In soft focus first behind the wire's diamond grid,

Then full focus as the fence wire fuzzes and fades.
There must be some significance in this image,
The reader, now viewer, assumes, since it stays so long onscreen.

The cars have an atmosphere of melancholy abandonment,
Left sitting all this time in the parking lot of a drab brick building
Which looks like the headquarters of some borderline business,

An insurance office, a chiropractor's, a miserable savings and loan.
And there may be something symbolic about the fence,
Holding in, as it did at first, the quintessential

American domestic automobile: indicating,
Perhaps, the confinement of contemporary marriage?
But this is all critical speculation, as the viewer is reminded

When the camera, without moving, drops
A frost-rotted crabapple from a high branch of the dark old tree
The cars sit under. It falls dead center

On a hood, and the viewer becomes
Listener: This film has sound, you realize.
Whang, the apple goes. Or does the hood go *thud*?

Whichever, the apple bounces now in artsy slow-motion
And the viewer notices the stain. Always the stain.
This is a different illusion, *the oracular illusion,*

As possible as any other. No accident
The one at Delphi was only a voice,
Untrustworthy, never accountable, never *I.*

Comme ça: *His grandmother used to say that.*
She got it from the Cajuns she grew up with
In South Louisiana, and for her it meant

Do it this way—not a good translation,
But he knew what she was saying. Eat your gumbo,
She'd tell him. Comme ça.

And she'd play-eat hers with a fork.
It was French, but it wasn't intellectual.
It was a joke. It was technique. It was rhetoric insofar

As it was persuasion. It worked.
Shrimp, crab, oyster:
He was landlocked, he didn't like those words.

They made him remember feelers and eyes and fish-stink cooking.
But sitting at the old walnut table
In her kitchen, he'd watch her, he'd giggle,

He'd eat. Out through the casement window, the camellia
Incandesced in March Louisiana sun,
And the live oaks dropped their old moss-strokes

From limb to limb to the ground.
We like to talk about remembering,
How everything assumes

Clarity at memory's center, no matter
That it fades to strange around the edges
Like the clichéd fly hung in nebulous amber:

Comme ça, *said his grandmother.*
She dipped her fork in his bowl, pretended to eat, and he
Ate truly: and though it was easier to swallow

While she did that, he still didn't like it.
It didn't seem fair to have to eat strange food
Just because he wasn't at home, just because the air

Through the window was dense with what he did not know
Was simple humidity: He could only see
It made everything different, an unfamiliar

Soup of a world. In his bowl, there were small sea creatures
He didn't want to think about, didn't want inside his body.
They reminded him of great depths, of subaqueous darknesses.

Comme ça, *his grandmother said, waving her fork.*
Do it this way. Do it this way.
And the red claw of camellia swam under fathoms of light.

VI

While that was happening, the woman wrestles
Her pale blue pullover off, drops it on the carpet.
She shrugs out of her brassiere, stands in a shaft of murky light

That comes down from the room's one small high window.
Her breasts are of medium size and have the slight sag
That reflects her middle age and signifies her children.

Her nipples are heavy and half-stiff, beginning now
To lift from large aureoles of indistinct roundness,
Permanently goosefleshed. *This is the clinical illusion.*

The man, in spite of any troubling questions
About time and verb tense and morality, is sitting in front of her.
He has found an honest straight-backed wheelless chair—

In that room full of objects designed for maximum efficiency
It seems old-fashioned, a miracle of domesticity—
And he sits fully clothed looking up at her.

His lips part. Will he speak? What will he say?
Language is magic, a technique, one
Which is born of desire, and which assures desire

Its being by means born of desire?
Who would he have to be to say such a thing?
Not who he is, not anybody he knows.

He holds out both hands like a deaf-mute signing,
Moves his palms on her breasts in gentle circles.
She understands. She steps closer to him

And he takes her left nipple into his mouth.
His tongue moves, and she speaks, she moans, and it means
Yes. Do it that way. Do it this way.

V I I

Always this sense that something is missing, always
This feeling there is something to be looked for
Blind, the way the newborn nuzzles for the mother's breast

And sucks that strange food down: This is the life in the body.
In December moonlight, a convertible circles the building,
Teenaged boys clichéd for love, thirsty. In the front seat,

One puts his hand in a sack, passes out tall cans of beer.
Aluminum shines under arclight, and the sudden foam
Hisses out of shaken cans onto their hands in the intervening
    darkness.

This is an image of masturbation or an image of the sea
Throwing itself with painless obsession
Against jagged and unyielding shorelines, this is an image of the
    seed

Of hyperbole or epic simile ready to uncoil
Out of the eight-cylinder rhythm of home-bored and -modified
    engines
And the hard certainty of horniness which is nothing but the root

Of the will to romance and the will to war and the will
To settle down and raise children quietly in the suburbs
After they appear suddenly in a life

Spent driving and drinking through streets at night
In a town you never asked to be born in, never liked the name of,
Never understood was the only town you could ever love

Because it prints itself hard-edged against the foam you turn into
While you beat yourself against it for years
Trying to wear it down, wear it away:

63

But it compensates perfectly, it accommodates itself
With quiet and infuriating unconsciousness to everything you do,
Takes the shape of your body, accepts your obsession

Without trouble or recognition, takes on your face
Easily, since you belonged to it in the first place
And it could not have been otherwise and can never be otherwise

No matter how fast and hard you drive
Dreaming of the bodies of teenaged girls who live
In houses so far from you

The machine that bears you would rust apart beneath you
Before you had traveled an nth part of the distance:
Your body would sink in the dust of its own going down.

VIII

The second-person illusion, *the intimate illusion,*
The illusion that drags you in.
You didn't want to be here. But nobody else did either,

And everybody has to be somewhere.
So this is Mt. Vernon, Ohio, and you are a stranger
In the sudden particularity of this secondary illusion, *fact.*

How real is it going to be, you want to know?
The incidents of this illusion are purely a fiction. The literal facts
Are chiefly connected with the natural and artificial

Objects and customs of the inhabitants. Which is to say, everything.
That's how the voice protects itself, that's how it lies to confuse
Your sense of who you are and where you are, that's how it makes
     you

Believe in the concrete reality of what is after all pure voice:
Claiming to remind you that none of this is real,
It lets you know in passing and underhandedly

That after all it *is*, and leaves you
To sort it out for yourself. In moonlight, Mt. Vernon, Ohio,
Is equivocal anyway, a town of antebellum houses and brick streets

And honky-tonks where the inhabitants shoot pool quietly.
They have their own objects and customs, these good Americans
Who never give a second thought to life in the heartland.

They work all week and on the weekends they drink, seldom get
     drunk,
And on Sunday they go to church in the morning, watch football
     all afternoon.
That's easy to say, and the voice is ashamed of itself

For the distance it can't help keeping from the inarticulate mystery
Of every human life. But what, after all, *are* the facts?
Somewhere in town, a husband and wife, pleasantly sleepy

From drinking a couple of beers while watching a TV movie,
Go to the bedroom, tune in a country-western station on the clock
    radio,
Make love satisfactorily but without great intensity,

Fall asleep. And that ought to be the whole story.
But in the middle of the night, one of them wakes up
To the sound of static: wakes with the weight of the body

Of a husband or wife heavy across his or her thighs,
Blood cut off: the flesh-tingle and the static
One thing, a voice without words, without human presence,

Omnipotent as death or human fate, which are one in the same—
And the one who wakes (the man or the woman? does it matter?)
    wants
To scream, it is so nightmarish to be awake in this half-dead body,

In this bedroom with another who is a sleeping stranger, unable to
    move,
Unable to reach the radio switch and stop that sound
Leaking from God knows where (out of the earth's

Magnetic field? out of the stars?) into the bedroom where the two
    of them lie
And have lied to each other and go on lying to themselves
In everything simple, in saying each other's names,

In saying *love* or *breakfast*, all that matters and does not matter,
And is nothing but the ongoing nothing
That wakes in the dark and hears that voice the radio makes

Present and out of reach, which is the voice
You can hear all over Mt. Vernon, Ohio, in the moonlight
If you are the *you* who has given yourself up

To this particular illusion. It is as if
The moonlight itself is hissing on the bricks
Of streets and houses, the godvoice behind everything.

At a party once, the woman tried to explain
A feeling she sometimes had that everything was falling apart.
"You mean spiritually, morally?" somebody asked. No:

She meant physically, and she meant *everything*.
She was a little drunk, and so were the others,
So explaining was hard. Finally somebody said,

"Yeah, the bomb," as if that settled the question.
Drinking, the woman considered: Maybe it *was* the bomb,
But right away she knew that was wrong. She had an image

Of how it would be when the bomb went off,
A soundless flash of angelic white, then blindness, burning.
This was different. This happened slowly, from within.

It made a noise like bricks scraping over bricks,
Like an engine throwing a rod, like somebody coughing up
   phlegm.
She had a feeling, though she did not know where it came from,

There was nothing new about it. She had a feeling
That sound had been around forever,
People had always heard it

But pretended not to, like now. "Put on some music," somebody
   said.
No, she wanted to tell them, *wait, listen*—
But too late. The stereo arm came down.

In the dark, in the office, in the straight-backed chair
The man lets the woman's nipple go, looks up.
Her head is tilted toward him, her long hair falls

Forward and down around her face, touches his.
Her hands cradle his head. One cups each ear gently.
He hears the small echo of air in the shells of her hands,

Hears the tick of her wristwatch, her breath, her heart,
A car with a bad muffler revving by in the street.
In that whole hierarchy of sounds, there is nothing he
    understands.

The stereo played Bill Monroe: "Blue Moon of Kentucky."
"Yeah," somebody said, "the High Lonesome Sound,"
And the host and hostess, drunk, leaned on each other, waltzing.

In the music, the high-pitched nervous plink of mandolin
Worried the stern three-quarter-time guitar,
A counterpoint emblematic of some old sorrow.

She looked at her husband. He sat across the table
Nursing a long beer, ready to go home.
And sometimes, those nights, she would look out the kitchen
    window

While the kids did homework in the other room or watched TV,
And imagine that once the whole surface of things ground itself
    away
There would be something underneath it, another world, angels,
    or light,

And she thought it would be worth it then, even if everybody
    died:
Just an instant of transparency. She touches the man's face.
He takes her breast again. It is some old reflex

Forgotten since infancy. He remembers how his wife would rub
    her nipple
On their newborn son's cheek to remind him how to nurse.
He remembers the sound of nursing, the sound of crying,

Remembers the high clear tenor voice on the radio—
Blue moon of Kentucky, keep on shining—
Remembers the circle of moon turning dark, turning light.

X

She is now so responsive to my kissing her breasts
That I can give her a climax in that way.
I still find it astonishing, miraculous, a gift

From the god of biology. As if the rest of it weren't enough.
Just when the body seems limited, insufficient: this.
Just when there needs to be more to touch, more parts of the body made

To correspond to touch, the nipples answer
Through surrender to this desire,
To this need that calls itself love.

So passion is a transfiguring force, something beyond
Delight and pain: beatitude?
But passion means suffering, a fact which we forget.

Which suffering comes next? Perhaps the hands
Will turn entirely sexual under this heat,
Perhaps touching hands will be all it will take.

And then perhaps the skin of the whole body.
Think of that: The lover's touch anywhere at all,
Or the touch of clothing, the simple touch of air,

Might be enough. And beyond that? The blood, the lungs?
So that one's very being, heartbeat and breath,
Might turn to a single lifelong climax, which we would not call

Sex any longer, but mystical pain, in which we would lose
Awareness of that which suffers, in which we would come,
Literally, at last, to understand?

It is a voice. It has a source.
I kiss her breasts, I touch her nipples with my tongue
And hear Jesus cry out on the cross.

Which heresy is this? Does it have a name?
Call it the heretic illusion if you have to call it:
When it comes to you, it is absolute authority, pure justification.

On the outskirts of Mt. Vernon, Ohio, the voice assumes
The foursquare shape of a cinder-block honky-tonk.
Inside, musicians tune instruments, warm up, run a sound check.

It's still a while until showtime. Nobody's in the bar
Except the bartender, two barmaids, and one hard-core
Old drunk, a constant customer. But the musicians are antsy,

Not nervous, exactly, but anxious, ready.
They sit at a small table in front of the bandstand. One
Has a mandolin, one a banjo, one a fiddle, one a guitar,

And they start to play an old hornpipe they won't do onstage,
Simple but intricate, unamplified, no good to two-step to.
Plainness, although simple, is not what I mean by simplicity.

Simplicity is a clean, direct expression of that essential
Quality of the thing which is the nature of the thing itself.
They play this for themselves, they play it for no one.

The drunk at the bar turns around to watch them.
From where he sits, he can see the soft shine
Of bar lights on the mandolin's mother-of-pearl.

The voice might have him think of anything now—
His mother, a lover, a good time in another town—
And say it is the music that guides his remembering,

That makes him suddenly happy or sad or angry or dissatisfied:
But this wouldn't do justice to the momentum of the inarticulate
Life that brings him here night after night

To drink cheap bourbon and purposely think about nothing.
There is a beauty in thinking nothing. It is more than
   simpleminded.
The musicians are thinking nothing. The fiddle player's eyes

Close as he gives his small life up to the life
Of Vassar Clements or Tommy Jarrell, to every hero of the fiddle
Whose wisdom is greater than his or any singular mind's.

The banjo player turns his hands into patterns
Evolved by generations of hands frailing the patterned
Necks of banjos. If he thinks, he drops the rhythm.

The drunk touches his glass. He is one of a long line
Of drunks. He can lose himself in tradition.
Later the band will play other, louder music

Onstage, and the bar will fill
With smoke and talk and the sexual odor of sweat,
And lovers will give up their lives

To the form of being lovers, and barmaids to the form
Of slapping the forms of the hands of solitary men
Pinching the lovely forms of buttocks drifting by.

But for now what they do they do quietly, in the spirit
Of meditation or prayer or gentle foreplay, their feet
Together tapping time's formality on the hardwood dance floor.

XII

Isn't it luminosity we are after?
Isn't it the high old style?
But the irony is, just at the critical juncture

She has to lower herself.
She stands in front of him, his right leg between her legs.
A small adjustment of her skirt lets her bare skin touch his pants.

She eases herself down. She feels him change
From her left breast to her right. She straddles him, she rocks,
    moans.
All utterance cherishes an object outside itself,

All words refer us to the world.
But who understands how? Is this *the objective illusion*?
Dull questions, in the face of which she clamps

Her legs around his leg and rises
To a more than rhetorical climax,
A tension easily aroused and satisfied,

Real enough, but not enough, a stopping point
On the way to the ultimate argument.
She holds his head in the dark between her hands,

Intuits, the way bodies can, the distance between
Her palms: It is so small
She suddenly wants to weep with pity and fear

At what that space contains.
She pulls him from her breast, tilts his face toward her.
All around them, the ominous

Shapes of the workplace gather.
She can see his face. She cannot see his face.
She wants to tell him something, but in her own head

The words sound sentimental, melodramatic, dangerous.
Their definitions have a sudden terrible clarity.
She kisses him, mouth open. She gives him her tongue.

Nothing but confusion has ever come
From the effort to fix the masculine/feminine boundary.
The opaque attitude proves useful for both.

Clarity? The moon: the arclight
Hung like its brighter reflection
High in the parking lot:

Milk-blue light that filters down
Through the small, high office window.
That's all clear enough,

Not man or woman or human but the world.
But in the opaque dark of the body,
Where we find ourselves and our story,

Such as it is, the slow old blood does its work.
She unbuttons his shirt, lays her hands
Against his chest, feels

His heart utter its simple repetitious word.
It refers to her. It refers her to herself.
That's what she's doing here, that's why her tongue

Moves itself in his mouth, that's why the dark
It moves in refuses to lighten to the syllable
That rises blind in the body: *name, name, name.*

XIII

Are you starting to get a feel for how the voice
Echoes? How *echo* here means motion in space *and* time?
It travels the way a lover's mumbled word crawls the arc

Of a domed building in India, a hundred yards along the wall
To the beloved, while nobody standing in the middle overhears a
   thing—
Or like the melodramatic stage whisper a woman hallucinates

In a low-budget movie when the director wants it understood
She's remembering something somebody said years ago.
The theory is, such motion is transcendence and thus salvation.

That's how it is with voices. The man, the voice can say,
Remembers, hears, anything at all the moment the woman lays
The satin whisper of her panties against his leg:

He embodies, for instance, in an instantaneous flash of imagistic
   recall,
The classroom at a state university twenty years ago,
A decrepit humanities building, a day in late September,

Hot Indian summer, all the windows open,
Everyone in the class half asleep in that late afternoon
While the teacher, a smartass graduate assistant,

Shows off what he knows about oracles.
Croesus, king of the Lydians, on the eve of going to war,
Inquired of the Delphic oracle what the outcome would be,

And was told: A great kingdom will fall, *which he did not take to mean*
His own. That's an old story, written somewhere in chapter one
Of the history of irony. Every college freshman learns it

Who stays awake in World Civilization 1-A.
The original Delphi was dedicated not
To the cult of Apollo, but to a female

Subterranean power, that of the great snake Delphyne,
Whose name conceals an archaic word for the womb.
Oracles are generally associated with the underworld,

And the oracle of Delphi was older than Apollo.
Can he really remember all that at such a moment?
Say *yes*—he can remember that and more:

The particular buzz of a particular fly twenty years dead,
One of a near-infinite line of flies stretching back
Into the world's impenetrable prehistory further back even than
   Delphyne,

Which flew into the stultified air of that classroom,
Black and heavy and itself half-asleep or half-dead
With the winter that the specialized sensitivity

Of its highly evolved body to certain death
Had to know was coming, Indian summer or no Indian summer:
His hand reaching up in a graceful clever motion

To snatch the fly alive out of the air
And contain the dull confusion of its buzzing
In a fly-sized flesh-hollow (he learned this trick

From his cousin on the farm, how easy it is
To catch flies in the air where they can't control
Even the tininess their own momentum is), and holding it,
   realizing

The power of life and death. The odds were fifty-fifty:
Kill it, let it go. Now let the oracle speak,
The oracle of flies, which this fly doubtless

Neglected to consult, or, if it did,
Received advice misleading, ambiguous, and dangerous.
If I kill this fly, he thought, *a great kingdom will fall.*

And now, of course, the voice is going to tell you
That no matter how detailed this memory is so far,
The man cannot for the life of him be sure

What came next. He can easily imagine that he opened
His hand in godlike mercy, or with equal ease that he flipped it
Floorward with a godlike wrist-snap of vengeance.

What does it matter? The fly died anyway.
The lesson? *The future is certain. It's the past
We can't be sure of.*

The woman moans, stiffens, coming.
O voice, O cheap and easy guide
To the inevitable, we bring you

Offerings, we pray you will explain
How the strange knotted taste of a nipple of flesh
Lives, and has its life in another life.

His hands are under her skirt. He touches nylon satin,
Touches skin. He knows muscle and bone, the highly evolved
And specialized body, come

Out of how many identical moments of the underworld
We call *time*, brought by how many accidental godlike touches
To this particular echo of *ekstasis*?

X I V

Where are we now? Have we even begun? The voice
Wonders at itself, moves in wonder at the way
It shapes the word it understands as love, moves to tell us

Mt. Vernon, Ohio, is a place of various edges:
Some shopping malls, some farms and orchards,
Some suburbs, some the local equivalent of slums,

But the churches all want to sit close to the center, where
They can build bell towers to toll out tunes territorial
As birdsong over the town square park. From here,

In the heart of *the blank verse illusion*, we can scan
Town square glowing in the hot illumination
Of floodlights the city fathers long ago

Saw the necessity of, to hold down sex
And violence—can see it from, as it were, a great height.
Again the high style. It would be easy now

To say this is Mt. Vernon's empty center,
This square, these sacred benches and trees
And sad wedding-cake fountain of whitewashed iron

Pissing up four inadequate streamlets from edges to heart—
Easy, but the voice resists. Sometimes even irony
Can be too simple. Look again. You forgot to see

The statue, the center of the center.
Everything else is submission to the fractured vision
Of the human world, which isolates everything you do—

Eating, dressing, earning money, making love—
And what is beyond? How can it all go on?
Don't you understand yet? This is the voice

Of desperation, looking for a method
To speak of these things without alienation, without scorn.
At the center of town square, as we see from our lonely height,

Is a statue, ordinary in material, subject, style:
Gray stone, a Civil War soldier abstract as Jesus,
Brother to a thousand others all over the country, North and South
    alike,

Its four-faced pedestal carved to quantify
History and passion, to name names but to tell no story.
In the center of Mt. Vernon, it lifts a countervoice:

East face:

ERECTED BY THE MOUNT VERNON
LADIES' MONUMENT ASSOCIATION
JULY 4, A.D. 1877

North face:

IN HONOR
OF THE VICTORIES
AND OF THE TRIUMPH
OF THE NATIONAL ARMS
IN THE WAR OF THE
GREAT REBELLION
1861–5
AND IN MEMORY
OF THE
NOBLE SONS OF KNOX COUNTY, OHIO,
WHO FOUGHT AND WHO FELL
IN THAT CONFLICT

West face:

"OUR COUNTRY!
BY THAT DREAD NAME WE WAVE THE SWORD ON HIGH,
AND SWEAR FOR HER TO LIVE—FOR HER TO DIE."

South face:

"DULCE ET DECORUM EST PRO PATRIA MORI"
IN GRATEFUL APPRECIATION OF THE
PATRIOTISM AND SELF-SACRIFICE OF THE

LAMENTED SONS AND SOLDIERS OF KNOX CO.
WHO FOR THEIR COUNTRY AND FOR FREEDOM
LAID DOWN THEIR LIVES IN THE WAR
OF THE GREAT REBELLION,
THIS MONUMENT IS ERECTED.
THEY LAID DOWN THEIR OWN LIVES THAT THE
LIFE OF THE NATION MIGHT BE PRESERVED, AND
SHARED IN THE GLORY OF SECURING TO EVERY
DWELLER IN THE LAND A HERITAGE OF HUMAN
FREEDOM: AND THEIR BLOOD HELPED TO CEMENT
THAT UNION, WHICH HAS MADE THIS
GREAT PEOPLE NOW AND FOREVER ONE.

It is the beaten countervoice of the human life
Of men and women in the United States of North America
And everything that means, the clichés and black holes

Of history and social theory, Manifest Destiny's urban sprawl
Gouged into stone, its line breaks predetermined
Not by prosody's arbitration but by the definite physical size

Of a six-ton chunk of granite bought and paid for
By charitable ministrations performed in the august name
Of the Mt. Vernon Ladies' Monument Association,

Its phrasing institutional and unconsciously sexual
As the soft white hands of Knox County wives knitting booties
To sell in service of mounting their heroic erection

In the center of Mt. Vernon, under the tritely phallic shadows
Of steeples, where now from the voice's unconscionable height,
We watch love-cars circle in arclight, drawn predictably as moths

To the flamelike stone soldier, whose face is so abstractly human
It is everyone's: and the boys in the white convertible forget
Their great rebellion as they drive, watching the shadowed park

For predestined women who exist nowhere except
In the conventional mind we all share, which insists this circling
Go on and on creating the life of what we call a nation,
    forever one:

79

Countervoice, reactionary echo thrown against storefronts, church
   doors,
Walls of houses where the righteous married carry on
Their fated and mythic domesticity:

Rhetoric thrown against the unyielding cold
Surface of statue-pedestal, circumventing every word
Of cynicism, irony, criticism, scorn, doubt,

Denying the existence of illusion, denying error and sin,
Obliterating the private life except as it gives itself up
Pro patria: voice and countervoice

Collide, cancel out, resurrect themselves,
Renew each other, wrestle toward death, desire each other
While the center of town trembles its silent detonation.

And above it all, over cartops and rooftops and treetops,
In that dark and ambiguous zone between biosphere and vacuum,
Moonlight shatters on an arctic cloud-mass blown

Due south under a sudden cold front filled with snow.
If we could define the physical world, if we knew what to call
Nature beyond that self-fulfilling and -defeating name,

We would have a language so pure it would require
No mind to contain it, no voice to speak it, no body
To breathe it out of its own air into its own air.

Language clearly either exists or does not exist
Without us. The way you think about it
Is a matter of pure faith, maybe, but the answer you choose

Determines everything. Listen: the moonlight coming down
From the small high office window suddenly changes.
The man, whose eyes are closed, does not notice.

He is kissing the woman's neck and shoulder gently
As he feels at her waist for skirt buttons. But the woman's
Eyes are open. She sees the light grown neither

More nor less but other in the room.
What does she think? The answer is complicated.
The man's tongue on her skin is a current of thought

That flows from her neck to her belly,
And his hands at her waistband are clumsy. She moves to help
   him
Reach higher on her throat and farther around her back

To points where nerves and buttons connect
At that moment of the shifting of the light.
Maybe she does not think anything. Maybe she thinks

His body is changing what her body thinks it sees.
She does not understand what is happening in the air
Between her retinas and the moon. Something out there

Has changed profoundly, but she cannot know that.
She touches the man's shirt buttons, opens his shirt,
Lays her palms on his chest. He shivers. Touching

His nipples, she touches the pit of his belly.
All things in the body are connected, all things in the air,
All things in our breath, but only as long as we breathe.

That's what the voice believes. But the voice is a voice.
It has a vested interest. So does the air, insofar as the light
It transmits is sunlight become moonlight become cloudlight

Filtered through the office window and through
The lenses and corneas and sensitive retinas
And unbelievably complex optic nerves and brain

Of what we call a woman, and back again
Through her neck and arms and hands
Into the chest of what we call a man

And down to the inward center of his belly
We call by no accident the *solar plexus*, which brings us
Full circle to the sun again, a trick

Of language justified only by the fact
That the man's hands finally solve the problem
Of the skirt's complexity of buttons, hooks, and zipper.

If you believe there are words without bodies, can you also believe
There are bodies without words? Nevertheless, whatever you
   believe,
The facts remain facts, as far as his hands can tell,

And they tell what they tell without saying that underneath
The wool skirt and beyond the elastic barrier
Of nylon satin, there lies sensitive flesh

Bicameral as the brain, as left- and right-lobed, equally
Mysterious, natural, named and unnameable, traditionally
Lunar, touched through his hands by his belly's solar light.

X V I

Summers, the boy's family would take him south
Through hardwoods, then pines, riverland, swampland,
Along mussel-shell roads serpentined by the Tangipihoa

Where his father said his mother's cousins night-poached alligators,
Wading waist-deep in moonlight with a flashlight and a knife.
He sat in the back seat watching the roadside, half visionary

And half bored, like anybody traveling, imagining
His friends at home, imagining his mother
When she was a girl, breaking the algaed surface

Of that river with her quick white body, diving. He'd seen
Old photographs of this same riverbank, of her
At fourteen in a swimsuit, rising from a homemade diving board,

A plank nailed to a rotted cypress stump,
The water she hung above in the black-and-white picture lead-silver,
Covered with gray lily pads and colorless scum.

Those pictures were an aperture into a half world he half understood:
The girl getting ready to dive was exactly his age,
And it was hard to think of her as his mother, hard

To know if he thought she was pretty or not. Her hair
Was long and hung wet: she'd been in already, down
Into whatever right-angled place the river's surface scum covered,

And he was still in the backseat, half carsick
And half in love. Grown up and remembering, he'd say
Such moments he was lost in time, thrown into a past

He never even lived: but that would be a lie.
He was not lost in his mother's or any past,
He was lost in the future. Live oaks, moss,

River stink on summer Louisiana wind:
All around him the present was falling apart
In the face of what in this boy was about to be

The human apocalypse of lust—but is not that quite yet,
So he does not call it that. He only thinks
Of the place by the river where that girl his mother

Lifted, wondering where she stood
As the mind of the camera catches her
Parting her legs in midair, her bad dive

Held timeless before the water
Can smack its lead-gray belly against her belly
If she's clumsy enough, or take her deep

Into the scum of itself, where everything that moves
Is feelered and goes where it goes
By pure flesh-hunger remembered against the current.

Comme ça: they touch, and the snow begins.
In the street, the convertible's window rises, closes its crack.
First you can hear the radio music, then you can't:

Blue moon of Kentucky, keep—
And if you're on the sidewalk and the car hisses past
At the instant of the window's closing, and if

You happen to know the song—*too many ifs*—
It will finish itself in your mind: *keep on shining,*
Shine on the one who's gone and left me blue—

The mind completes what it knows, the old clichéd
Rhyme of the history of unhappy love, lifted over
A fiddle and mandolin by a voice

Like a dog caught in a barbed-wire fence, the High Lonesome
    Sound:
Blue moon of Kentucky, keep on shining,
Shine on the one who's gone and proved untrue.

The trick of the song is memory: The trick is to keep
The mind just far enough, but not too far,
From cliché, the fossil history of the heart;

From happy love, which has no history; from romance,
Which comes into existence only
Where love is fatal, frowned on

And doomed by life itself.
In the office, the man and woman touch.
Is it enough to say they touch? Will the circle

Of this memory intersect other circles
So that something independent reveals itself?
The man and woman reveal each other:

They touch, then they do not touch.
The man takes off his shirt. The woman
Stands up, and her loose skirt slides

Down the satin of her panties. She steps out.
Arclight through the window deepens into snowlight
And the woman stares at the man's goose-fleshed chest.

The foot of air between them seems so far
She thinks if she reached for him now, she would fall
Into one of the clichés of adultery,

Which has as long a history as possession.
This, she thinks, *is an affair*. She's never had one.
She finds a terror in the word

She could hardly have imagined would be there:
Not the fear of being caught, but of being trite.
This is one of those soap operas she hates.

This is a boring story in a magazine
On a rack in a grocery store.
This is a worn-out joke.

She puts her hands over her nipples
In a gesture of sudden shame
And starts to turn away—but the man

Lays his palms on her belly.
The heat she feels is traditional, and compels her
To touch his face, because it is a force so much

Larger and more enduring than she is.
What she has found is sure
Evidence of a connection in being human

Which everybody knows but nobody names
Without irony, or terror of the pure cliché,
Except here, where the woman bends to the man

And uncovers her breasts again, and puts her hands
On his hands on her belly, and kisses him while the snow
Crystallizes in the arclit air outside

And the convertible makes its circuit of the square
Holding that old rhyme, repeating,
Completing its strict music inside itself.

Outside, the sky and its moon wiped vacant and darkly clean
By massed snow clouds, and the street slicked
With a film of something nameless, neither snow nor ice,

And the cars in the parking lot laminated three shades paler,
And the velocity of the rot in the crabapple brought near
The vanishing point by sudden cold—outside, the voice

Remembers its way to the edge of Mt. Vernon, Ohio, to the
    roadhouse
Where now the band is playing. The fiddler stands
In a cone of cobalt brilliance shot

Down at his face from an ancient spotlight: Sweat
Glitters unnaturally on his forehead and cheeks, touched
With the depth of that blueness, a color

Not found in the sky or the sea:
And by whatever art it is that a man conveys
His character and sense of himself to the world, he stands

Alone where the circle of his memory intersects
Everything, where the circle stands unbroken
Where it matters, in the strength of its internal law—

Playing, in other words, the fiddle
For the people who are there now, who have come for this.
He plays a tune they all know, but that only he knows

The way he knows it: It is theirs, it is his,
Nobody in the room cares who it belongs to, as long
As it comes to them sweet and hot and they have enough beer.

Outside the cold gets colder, there are no visible stars,
The wind comes down from a circle of its own making.
How can the voice justify the world to the world,

The hard, impenetrable backdrop of the inhuman
With the song that fiddler bows?
Comme ça: Outside the roadhouse, let's say, a white convertible
   stops.

Its doors open. The music it carried is off.
Inside, in the crowd, a man stands up, one who belongs there:
He has on Levi's and Dingo boots, a plaid cowboy shirt

With opalescent snaps and a silver thread in the weave,
A wide leather belt with a gold steer forged on the buckle,
A white Stetson hat. He goes onstage, takes a microphone,

The move perfectly casual, random, perfectly planned.
When he turns to the crowd and sings, he is precisely
On cue and pitch: And as the first words

Of the song come out of the PA system,
Four underage men stumble in through the fake swinging doors
And hear it again: *Blue moon of Kentucky, keep—*

This is *the illusion of wonder, the illusion of synchronicity,*
The déjà vu illusion: It is as though the song
Has followed them, or come out of them, and they stand

Reverent in the door of the roadhouse, grinning
At this welcome, or in the amazed shame
Of one who is suddenly loved and suddenly knows it.

XIX

I remember the summer, the dense green shade of the yard,
The old brick house my grandmother lived in, crumbled
By roots of long-suffering ivy and Louisiana mildew.

I was the boy half dead of boredom, of entropy of the soul,
Who circled the lawn catching chameleons in the depth of bamboo hedge,
Insufferable. I suffered myself. I was there.

What was happening in my heart? I could have told you
It hurt. I could have told you I was in love
With something, every second, I did not know how to name

Much less touch. I think I could have said
When egrets lifted into the sky of my grandmother's yard
From the green-scummed water of the Tangipihoa

I hated them for their whiteness, for the light
Lift of their wingspan, for how they wheeled and vanished.
Everything I loved went on without me.

And when girls walked past on the white oyster-shell road,
I hid in the cool bamboo and spied on their breasts'
New vibration and thrust behind T-shirts. Translucence:

That was the word I did not know, but needed.
I could not have told you how it hurt me to hate
The half-seen hunched-at shapes of the naturally hidden,

To wake from an unremembered dream in the crotch-slick
Louisiana night, humid in the groin with the knowledge
That something I could not name had almost touched me:

I hated the pain in my body, I hated my body,
I hated loving whatever it was I loved.
This was the end of my natural life,

The end of living the way small animals live
In the womb of grass or water.
I hated what I was born from, earth, mother, father.

I hated imagination, which always outstripped my distinctions,
Which lifted the blinding T-shirts of girls, turned them and me
Inside out. That's just growing up, you say.

Oh, it's all perfectly natural.
That's why I was a boy, that's why it was Louisiana,
That's why the egrets floated paired in the sexual air,

That's why, when I found, at the back
Of my grandmother's closet,
A paperback copy of a book

With the cover ripped off and read
Of the man's throbbing velvet shaft
And the woman's honeyed hole

And the sweetness of the flowing
Juices and the good hurt
Of bodies about to be touched,

I knew I loved
One nature and not another,
Some man's unimaginable daughter,

Knew those words were not what I was, but what I was
Fated to become, countervoice, the ancient argument:
That the body is a way of knowing.

That nerves and skin are one authority
No one sane and living
Will argue with seriously

When it comes right down to the question
Of pain's reality.
That when you kick the stone

The voice you assume
Comes out of your gut so sudden
You forget you believe you subsume

Body in your personal Oversoul.
Let that formal feeling come.
Let the man and the woman feel

Imperiously drawn
To the same voice, to the real
Negation of what they think they own

And will not in this life give up owning.
Let them come anyway, not knowing they come
Blind to each other, built to know by touching

And knowing by touching's pain
That nothing is only nothing,
That the voice owns everything.

X X

Now, in the parking lot, miraculously, snow
Precipitates from the air, turns the pair of cars
Left there into beautiful abstractions.

The night inflates with the luminosity of snowfall,
Dim but tangible. The edges of the ugly
Office building harden against what is not sky

But eddies and lacy jags of snowfall suspended
Between you and the actual sky, an illusion of sky
Appearing and falling out some indeterminate middle distance

No sense of perspective can define. But notice: You
Are here now. The voice has brought you
Obliquely, sucked you in and surrounded you

With a world disappearing as you watch it
Into soft, stark undifferentiation.
This is an act of will. This is a leap of faith.

This is a godlike power that lets you penetrate
Space, mind, time, the brick walls of an office building
You never wondered about before, wherein

The man and the woman face each other.
You move, the walls dissolve, you see her stand
Naked, finally, before him.

The voice holds them for you motionless in a light
Bizarre as X-ray illumination, or an infrared
That lets you see the metaphysically disguised,

But is, after all, only the refracted whiteness
Of snowfall come down through a small high office window.
Yet for now, the scene seems timeless, like a drawing on a wall

Of a cave deep beneath the surface of France, touched suddenly
By the flashlight glow and carbon-14-sensitive instruments
Of archaeologists come to witness and record,

Come to try to understand that when masculine figures appear
    here
They are always clothed in some sort of costume,
But these female figurines are absolutely naked,

Simply standing, unadorned. This, they conjecture,
Says something about the psychological and consequently mythical
Values of the male and female presences: The woman

Is immediately mythic in herself
And is experienced as such,
Not only as the source and giver of life,

But also in the magic of her touch and presence.
Whereas the male, costumed, is one
Who has *gained* his powers

And represents some specific, limited,
Social role or function. The man, in fact, is costumed.
He has his pants and shoes on—

Levi's, deck shoes from L. L. Bean—chosen carefully to fit
His sense of years of living to gain and own
Himself, this particular man come to be

Husband somehow, father somehow, respectable businessman,
A good man somehow, a nice man somehow, somehow
    responsible and kind,
And now somehow about to be the lover

Of this woman who stands before him naked,
And in this connection suddenly the clothes he still wears seem
Absurd, inappropriate, an insult

To the presences he senses around him—the woman,
The archaeologists with their flashlights,
The voice, and especially *you*,

94

The illusion who has come here expecting something—so he
   stands,
Kicks off the shoes easily, bends to slip off the socks,
Struggles for a moment with belt buckle and Levi's button and
   zipper,

Wrestles the jeans off, slips out of the jockey shorts,
Straightens, and faces the woman.
He is taller than she is, a little. Millions of years

Of natural selection have seen to that. Millions of generations
Have brought them here in their different bodies,
And in their nakedness they assume the dignity

Of biological tradition, whose marks are everywhere
On the flesh which possesses them: shape of the penis erect,
Receiving shape of the vagina, shape of the hands

Made to grip, stroke, penetrate: shape of the nerves
Of the skin made ubiquitous, sensitive, inflammable.
Here everything the body is stands effective and revealed

And if she does not think, *But I hardly know him*
It is because she is in this relation to him,
Having dropped and scattered everything

Concealing, everything temporal, everything temporary
As home, husband, children—revealing herself
Continuous with the powers we name *light, life, passion*—

In which continuum she knows him perfectly. And he
Does not think anything, having thrown away
The emblems of what he thinks of as himself:

He touches her with the absolute authority
The body, revealed, reveals. History, mythology,
Biology, the art of the family

Suspend as the man and woman move together.
And that might be all, that might be the end of the story
If the voice chose to let you forget

The truth: that this is the workplace, that you are here
To witness everything, beginning to end,
And since you have given yourself up

To this, *the passionate illusion*, you can only go into the body
Of the act, into the reality of consequence,
Into the life of that slice of the natural world

We choose to call *Mt. Vernon, Ohio*,
Within which and outside of which
Everything that happens here happens.

So now, the man and woman touch and come together
And the egg in her body is ready for the sperm in his,
And maybe their natural children are sleeping in different rooms

Across town from each other, dreaming of a place
Where snow falls and dissolves in the black silence of a stream
That follows itself under winter-dead trees coldly toward the sea.